THIS WALKER BOOK BELONGS TO:

_____

_____

_____

For Agnes from me, and
for Holly from the
elephants
M.J.

For all of George's
grandmas, Hazel, Kathy,
Pauline and Gillian
I.B.

First published 2003 by Walker Books Ltd
87 Vauxhall Walk, London SE11 5HJ

This edition published 2004

10 9 8 7 6 5 4 3 2 1

Text © 2003 Martin Jenkins
Illustrations © 2003 Ivan Bates

This book has been typeset in Cheltenham and Shinn

Printed in China

British Library Cataloguing in Publication Data:
a catalogue record for this book
is available from the British Library

ISBN 1-84428-726-2

www.walkerbooks.co.uk

GRANDMA ELEPHANT'S IN CHARGE

Martin Jenkins

illustrated by
Ivan Bates

WALKER BOOKS
AND SUBSIDIARIES
LONDON • BOSTON • SYDNEY • AUCKLAND

Most elephants live in families. And most elephant families are **big** (just like elephants).

Elephants are the biggest land
animals of all. A big male
can weigh six tonnes –
as much as 100 people.

There'll probably be two or three babies,
forever playing push-me-pull-you, or peekaboo,
or anything else that makes a lot of noise.
And each of the babies might have an older brother
or sister – handy for playing king of the castle on!

Elephant mothers have only one baby at a time.
They give birth every three or four years.
Elephants don't become fully grown until
they're ten years old or more.

The mothers in the herd are usually sisters.

Adult male elephants don't normally stay with the family. Instead they move about by themselves or with other males.

And then there are the mums. They look after their own babies, and each other's too – keeping an eye on them to make sure they don't wander off, and scolding them when they get too boisterous.

But that's not all. The most important member of an elephant family is ...

11

Grandma!

Elephants can live for up to
sixty-five years, but don't
usually have any more babies once
they're older than fifty or so.

Grandma's been around a long time and she knows lots of important things. She knows where the water holes are when it hasn't rained and the easiest places to cross the big river when it has rained.

Elephants move around a lot.
It's important for them to have good
memories so that the family doesn't get
lost when they return to
places they haven't visited
for a very long time.

She knows where to find the juiciest melons ...
and knows the best path up the cliff to the salt lick.
It's not surprising that she's the one in charge.

Elephants are very fond of things like melons but feed mainly on grass,
leaves and twigs. Adults eat about 1.5 tonnes of food each day.

Salt licks are places where the earth is full of minerals. Lots of animals eat
the minerals, which help to keep them healthy.

She doesn't make a big song-and-dance about it, though. Just a flick of the ear or a snort or two, and a **rumble, rumble, rumble,** deep down in her throat, seem to be enough to tell all the other elephants what to do.

If she stops, they all stop. If she moves, they all move. And if there's any sign of danger, you can be sure she'll be the first to investigate and the first to decide what the family should do.

They might all run away...
or they might take a stand.

21

Or Grandma might **c-h-a-r-g-e**.
If she charges with her head up and ears
flapping, waving her trunk and making
a great to-do, then she's probably bluffing.

But if her head's down, her trunk's
tucked under and she's not making
any noise, then she means business.
In that case, whatever it is that has
annoyed her had better watch out.

A charging elephant can
run at 40 kph – that's faster
than the fastest human.

And once all the commotion's over,
everyone can settle back down to feeding
and snoozing and messing about – safe in
the knowledge that Grandma has sorted
things out again.

So if you're an elephant,
there's one thing you should
never forget. Wherever you
are and whatever you're doing,

**Grandma's
in charge!**

ABOUT ELEPHANTS

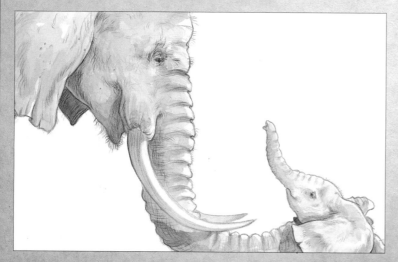

There are two kinds of living elephant. The elephants in this book are African elephants; the other kind are Asian elephants, which live in South and South-east Asia. Elephants were once found almost everywhere in Africa, but now they have disappeared from many of the places where they used to live. This is because they have been hunted and people have taken their land for farming. Twenty years ago there were over 1,000,000 African elephants. Now there may be only half that number.

Index

Look up the pages to find out about all these elephant things. Don't forget to look at both kinds of word –

this kind and this kind.

About the author

Martin Jenkins is a conservation biologist and author of the award-winning *The Emperor's Egg,* amongst other children's books. Martin has seen wild elephants many times, but the first time he saw them was in Kenya. "There was a big family of them making their way across the savanna," says Martin. "I'll never forget them, strolling across the plains without a care in the world – it was magic."

About the illustrator

Ivan Bates has illustrated a number of children's books, including *Do Like a Duck Does.* About this book, Ivan says, "I have always found elephants fascinating creatures capable of both extreme strength and tenderness. This combined with their almighty stature and set in those wonderful, vast land and skyscapes, makes them a joy to draw."

NOTES FOR TEACHERS

The READ AND WONDER series is an innovative and versatile resource for reading, thinking and discovery. Each book invites children to become excited about a topic, see how varied information books can be, and want to find out more.

Reading aloud The story form makes these books ideal for reading aloud – in their own right or as part of a cross-curricular topic, to a child or to a whole class. After you've introduced children to the books in this way, they can revisit and enjoy them again and again.

Shared reading Big Book editions are available for several titles, so children can read along, discuss the topic, and comment on the different ways information is presented – to wonder together.

Group and guided reading Children need to experience a range of reading materials. Information books like these help develop the skills of reading to learn, as part of learning to read. With the support of a reading group, children can become confident, flexible readers.

Paired reading It's fun to take turns to read the information in the main text or in the captions. With a partner, children can explore the pages to satisfy their curiosity and build their understanding.

Individual reading These books can be read for interest and pleasure by children at home and in school.

Research Once children have been introduced to these books through reading aloud, they can use them for independent or group research, as part of a curricular topic.

Children's own writing You can offer these books as strong models for children's own information writing. They can record their observations and findings about a topic, make field notes and sketches, and add extra snippets of information for the reader.

Above all, Read and Wonders are to be enjoyed, and encourage children to develop a lasting curiosity about the world they live in.

Sue Ellis, Centre for Language in Primary Education